MRJC
5/14

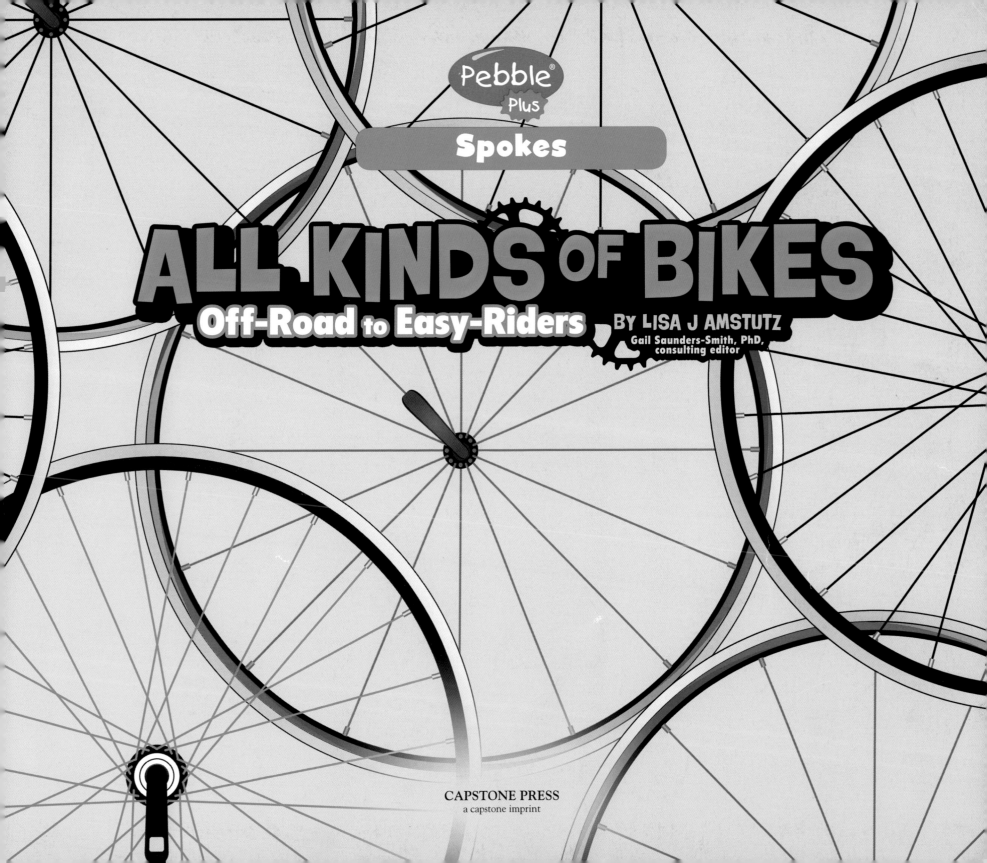

Pebble® Plus

Spokes

ALL KINDS OF BIKES
Off-Road to Easy-Riders

BY LISA J AMSTUTZ

Gail Saunders-Smith, PhD,
consulting editor

CAPSTONE PRESS
a capstone imprint

Pebble Plus is published by Capstone Press,
1710 Roe Crest Drive, North Mankato, Minnesota 56003.
www.capstonepub.com

Library of Congress Cataloging-in-Publication Data
Amstutz, Lisa J.
All kinds of bikes: off-road to easy-riders / by Lisa J. Amstutz.
pages cm.—(Pebble Plus. Spokes)
Includes bibliographical references and index.
Summary: "Full-color photos and simple text introduce different styles of bicycles"—Provided by publisher.
ISBN 978-1-4765-3967-6 (library binding)
ISBN 978-1-4765-6030-4 (ebook pdf)
1. Bicycles—Juvenile literature. I. Title.
TL412.A67 2014
629.227'2—dc23
                                    2013031427

Editorial Credits
Jeni Wittrock, editor; Kyle Grenz, designer; Jennifer Walker, production specialist; Sarah Schuette, photo stylist; Marcy Morin, photo scheduler

Photo Credits
Alamy: Tim sport, 9; Dreamstime: Carlos Santos, 17, Juriah Mosin, 21; Getty Images: Stone/Andre Gallant, 5, Taxi/Jordan Siemens, 7, Workbook Stock/Mark A Johnson, 13; Glow Images: Cusp/Corbis/Steve Prezant, 19; iStockphotos: AnastasiyaShanhina, 11; Newscom: Image Broker/Jim West, cover; Shutterstock: Jacek Chabraszewski, 15

Design Elements:
Shutterstock: filip robert, Kalmatsuy Tatyana

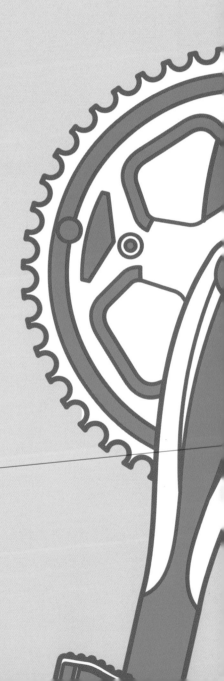

Note to Parents and Teachers

The Spokes set supports national standards related to physical education and recreation. This book presents and illustrates types of bicycles. The images support early readers in understanding the text. The repetition of words and phrases helps early readers learn new words. This book also introduces early readers to subject-specific vocabulary words, which are defined in the Glossary section. Early readers may need assistance to read some words and to use the Table of Contents, Glossary, Read More, Internet Sites, and Index sections of the book.

Printed in the United States of America in North Mankato, Minnesota.
092013   007775CGS14.

Table of Contents

Let's Go!

Some bikers love to race. Others cruise off the paved path. Some riders do daring stunts. For every kind of rider, there is a bike to match.

City Bikes

Road bikes are perfect
for short trips around town.
Thin tires zip over streets.
Riders switch gears to make
it easy to pedal uphill.

Track bikes are light
and fast. Riders race
them on indoor tracks.
Disc wheels slice through
the air for more speed.

Take Your Time

Touring bikes are made
for long bike trips.
Their frames are light
but strong. They can carry
water bottles and bags.

Riders sit low to the ground

on recumbent bikes.

These bikes are comfortable

for long rides. Riders lean

back in their seats.

No Roads

Not all bikes need roads
or tracks. A mountain bike
travels in the country.
The bike's wide, bumpy tires
grip rough trails.

BMX bikes fly over tracks

with ramps. These bikes have

stunt pegs. While doing

tricks, riders can stand

on the pegs or the pedals.

peg

Even More Bikes

Not all bikes have two wheels.

Bikers with good balance can

ride one-wheeled unicycles.

Tricycles have three wheels.

They are hard to tip.

Want to bike with friends?

A multibike seats three

or more people. Or take one

friend on a tandem bike.

It is built for two!

Glossary

balance—the ability to stay steady and not fall over

disc wheel—a light but solid wheel for a bike; disc wheels help indoor racers go faster

gear—a round, toothed part of a bike that turns the tires; different gears make it easier to push a bike's pedals

grip—to hang on tight

pave—to cover with a hard surface like cement or tar

recumbent bike—a comfortable kind of bicycle that is built to allow the rider to lean back in the seat

stunt—a trick that shows great skill or daring

stunt peg—a tube attached to the wheel of a BMX bike; the rider can stand on the peg or balance it on a ledge

Read More

Hamilton, Robert M. *On a Bike.* Going Places. New York: Gareth Stevens Pub., 2012.

Herrington, Lisa M. *Bicycle Safety.* Rookie Read-About Safety. New York: Children's Press, 2012.

Mara, Wil. *What Should I Do? On My Bike.* Community Connections. Ann Arbor, Mich.: Cherry Lake Pub., 2012.

Internet Sites

FactHound offers a safe, fun way to find Internet sites related to this book. All of the sites on FactHound have been researched by our staff.

Here's all you do:

Visit *www.facthound.com*

Type in this code: 9781476539676

Index

Word Count: 209
Grade: 1
Early-Intervention Level: 16